Learning the History of Kelley Park in San Jose

Paul Trainer
Edited by Leonard McKay

Order this book online at www.trafford.com
or email orders@trafford.com

Most Trafford titles are also available at major online book retailers.

Print information available on the last page.

ISBN: 978-1-4120-6895-6 (sc)
ISBN: 978-1-4907-7318-6 (e)

Trafford rev. 05/06/2016

Trafford
PUBLISHING® www.trafford.com
North America & international
toll-free: 1 888 232 4444 (USA & Canada)
fax: 812 355 4082

Learning the History of Kelley Park in San Jose

The Lord walks not only in front and behind me.
He rises above and watches where he leads me.

Paul Trainer

Sometimes when I look at my son I see him struggling,
trying and wanting to become a man and I also see
his sadness knowing he will never be a child again.

Paul Trainer

This is the first book of its kind to be written with special
places of family interest and these animated characters.
This book is dedicated to teachers, students, children, hospitals,
institutions, educational programs, care centers, libraries,
historians, schools, bookstores and non-profit organizations.

✝ **And to My Father**
Paul Arthur Trainer
A Man who loved his Wife and Family
Oct. 3, 1920—Aug. 26, 2005
A New Life Begins

Books order information at
www. prtproductions.com

Special thanks to Leonard McKay for his expertise
on not only writing, but for his approval of this book.

Happy Hollow

Archer House

Japanese Friendship
Gardens

History Park

Lawrence Archer was a San Jose lawyer and twice mayor of the city

The original Archer home burned in 1909. After the house was rebuilt, Louise Archer Flavin Kelley, left, lived in it for 40 years.

San Jose Mercury News ■ September 29, 1982

Thirty-one years ago, the city of San Jose acquired 63 acres of a country estate on the west bank of the Coyote Creek. City officials called it Kelly Park after the woman who sold it to the city. And they put in a zoo, a children's play area, a community-center building, the Japanese Friendship Garden, a historical museum, picnic areas and train rides. Today it is the subject of controversy. Marine World-Africa USA likes the looks of the parcel on the east side of Coyote Creek off Senter Road and Capitol Expressway. Residents in the area like the park the way it is - peaceful and without the baying of lions and honking traffic. Few know the history of the place they call Kelley Park. When it was sold for $142,000, it was going to be named Archer Park. Louise Archer Flavin Kelley hoped that it would be called after her maiden name. Instead, the city chose to name it Kelley. In an interview in August 1951, Mrs Kelley, then 88, told me her father bought the original 160 acres in 1861 and moved the family from its large residence at Fountain and Second streets in 1869. She was then 6 years old. In 1951, she had lived in the home for 40 consecutive years, working in the extensive gardens and devoting her energies to landscaping and improving the estate. She was the daughter of Lawrence Archer, distinguished San Jose lawyer, twice mayor of the city, one-time county judge and member of the state legislature.

Archer, a native of South Carolina, practiced law in Mississippi. In 1843, he became the pioneer lawyer in the new little frontier community of St. Joseph on the Missouri River. The next year, he was elected district attorney, serving until May 1852, when he joined a wagon train bound for California. He settled in San Jose in January 1853 and almost immediately became involved in the city's affairs. He was elected mayor in 1856 and again in 1878; served as county judge from 1868 to 1871; was a member of the state assembly in 1875; member of the first Board of Regents of the University of California; and a member of the state Board of Normal School Trustees. The Archer building stood at 32 S. Second St. for many years and was finally torn down to make room for a parking lot. Judge Archer had his law offices in another building he owned at First and Santa Clara streets, according to Mrs. Kelley, who also remembered that the town pump was at First and Fountain (formerly known as Archer Alley) streets. Judge Archer called his country estate (in Kelley Park) Lone Oak, and in later years when his daughter made her home there, it was called Arc-Kel Villa for the Archer-Kelly families. The judge planted 40 acres in cherries and other fruits and landscaped the acres around the two-story home. The house in which the judge died and in which Mrs. Kelly lived for 40 years is used for storage, ranger offices and recreation programs. This house replaced the original, which burned in May 1909. The new house had only been completed one day when judge Archer died Feb. 17, 1910. He was the father of three children. Mrs. Kelley was a daughter by his first wife, and Lawrence and Leo (the latter a prominent San Jose attorney) were sons by his second wife. Little Miss Archer grew up in San Jose and graduated from the old San Jose Normal School with the class of 1881.

Two years later, she married Martin J. Flavin, a San Francisco businessman, in an elaborate wedding held in the Archer home. The wedding filled more than two columns on page 1 of The San Jose Daily Mercury, the lists of guests taking up more than half the space. The society reporter pulled out all the stops in describing both the bride and groom, as well as the beauty of the setting with an abundance of punctuation marks. Flavin died a few years later, and Louise Archer Flavin married Frank J. Kelley, founder of the Star-Peerless Wallpaper Mills in Chicago Ill.

The couple went to Chicago to live, but on the death of her father, Mrs. Kelly returned to make her home permanently on the country estate. She was the mother of four sons, Frank J. Kelley Jr.; Dr. Kenneth Kelley, Lawrence A Kelley; and Martin Flavin, Pulitzer Prize-winning author. Mrs. Kelly sold the estate to two San Jose public-spirited businessmen, Ernest H. Renzel and Alden Campen, who agreed to act as the city's agents at no cost to the city.

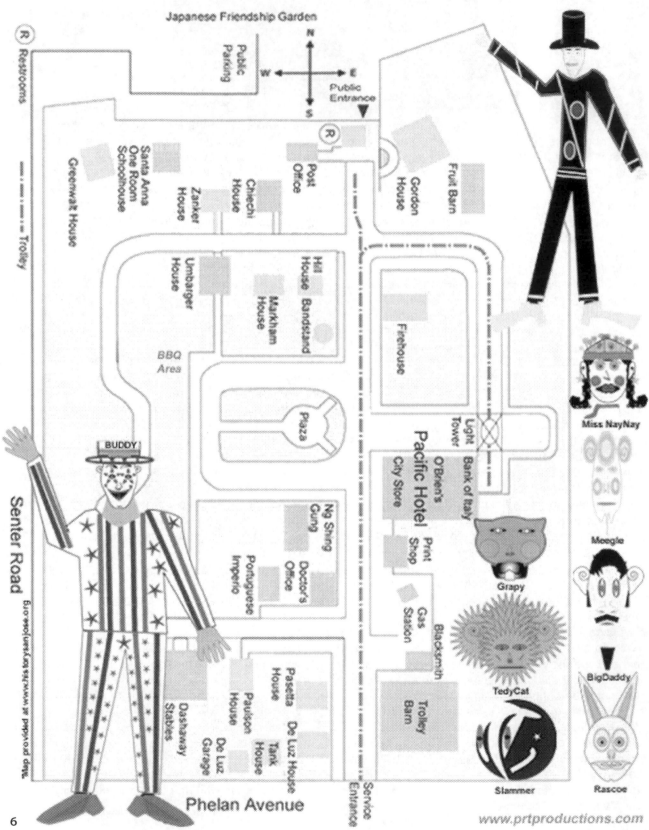

Japanese Friendship Garden

N
W   E
S

Public Parking

Public Entrance

R   Restrooms

Trolley

Greenwalt House

Santa Anna One Room Schoolhouse

Zanker House

Chiechi House

Post Office

R

Fruit Barn

Gordon House

Umbarger House

Hill House Bandstand

Markham House

Firehouse

BBQ Area

Plaza

Light Tower

Bank of Italy

O'Brien's City Store

Pacific Hotel

Miss NayNay

Meagle

Grapy

BigDaddy

TedyCat

Senter Road

BUDDY

Ng Shing Gung

Doctor's Office

Portuguese Imperio

Print Shop

Gas Station

Blacksmith

Trolley Barn

Slammer

Rascoe

Dashaway Stables

Paulson House

Pasetta House

De Luz House Tank House

De Luz Garage

Service Entrance

Phelan Avenue

6

Hello everyone and welcome. My name is Buddy and this is my friend Mr. Disbig.
The History Park is located at the south end of Kelly Park, then you have the
Japanese Friendship Garden in the center, and at the north end you have Happy Hollow.
These three parks are different from each other, and yet, very special in their own way.
Along with a few of our friends, you will be receiving a fantasic tour around these parks.
We will begin with History San Jose, also known as HSJ. I would like to bring your
attention to the map. Now if any kids are helping your parents read, maybe you could
tell them what directions to take. We will be starting at the South (back) Gate, which is
the service entrance, then moving West up to the North (main) Gate and coming
back around toward the East. We will eventually end up back where we
started. But first, let me tell you a little about how the History Park was started.

1963 - Museum concept adopted by Historic Landmarks Commission

1964 - Historic Landmarks Commission visits Kern County's Museum's
Pioneer "Village" type Museum. Council turns down request on advice from
Director of Parks and Recreation, Planning Commission, and City Manager.

1965 - Historic Landmarks Commission with help from Department of
Public Works (Architectural Engineering) lays out a proposed town site
at Kelly Park. First attempt by Historic Landmarks Commission to have a
Museum Director position put into the city's budget. Unsuccessful.

1966 - Historic Landmarks Commission compiles a list of buildings that would
be suitable to move into proposed historical town site. Second attempt by Historic
Landmarks Commission to have a museum Director put into the city's budget.
Unsuccessful.

1967 - City buys Bohnett Collection of antique autos, motorcycles, animal-
drawn carriages, amusement machines, dolls, dishes, clothes, etc...
from Trader Lew Bohnett for $235,000. Mr. Theron Fox, Landmarks
President, made the deal for the city. Mr. Earnest Renzel put up the cash
for the collection and the city paid Mr. Renzel $50,000 per year. Third
attempt by Historic Landmarks Commission to have a museum Director
put into the city's budget. Unsuccessful.

1968 - City builds two steel warehouses to take care of Bohnett Collection
and other artifacts for future Museum. Forth attempt by Historic Landmarks
Commission to have a museum Director put into the city's budget. Unsuccessful.

1969 - Museum Directors position approved for 1969-1970 budget. Mr. John
B. Dowty appointed Director in September of 1969. Plans begun for a "Village"
type Museum on 16- acre plot at south end of Kelley Park.

1970 - Work begun on site for outdoor museum (old San Jose 1850-1920) in October.
Dennis Peterson apointed curator.

1971 - Statehouse Museum closed- plans begun to build museum in south warehouse.
New Museum opened to public June 18, 1971.

The Statehouse Museum opened in 1950 and was located at the Santa Clara Fairgrounds.
And that was in the beggining. Now let's turn the next page and dive into the past where
we will find a beautiful peaceful park filled with squirrels, birds and an ocassional turkey.
We might even see the trolley running and I know we will see many beautifully restored
buildings through the behalf of donations, staff and honored volunteers.

This is the DeLuz house, Mr. Disbig. It was at 502 S. 11th Street in downtown San Jose many years ago. Kristena Nelson Deluz wanted the house brought here after she died. Did you know she was a professor at San Jose State University?

No. I didn't know that, Buddy. Did you know it is now the home of the Hellenic Heritage Institute? The home was built about 1905 and was moved here in 1987.

Wow. Inside, Mr. Disbig, are beautiful paintings and artifacts representing Greek culture. Sometimes they have seminars, cooking and dancing classes and have parties here at HSJ.

That's fantastic, Buddy. Isn't that the renovated Pasetta House next door. I here they have 30 or more paintings from San Jose's best known-artists.

They do, Mr. Disbig. The Pasetta house used to be at St. James and Terraine Streets. It was built in 1905. A Yugoslavian couple owned a fruit-drying business and raised nine children in the home. The home was moved to History Park in 1985.

The sign out front reads, The Leonard and David McKay Gallery, Buddy. Leonard Mckay collected paintings and sold some to benefactor Rob Bettencourt. I think the Pasetta House at History Park is the perfect place to show such a fine collection of artistry.

I agree with you, Mr. Disbig. Let's cross the street and check out the Doctor's house.

I think I need a doctor, Buddy. For some reason I've lost all my color. Matter of fact, my clothes are even black and white. I don't feel so well. I think I might faint.

10

Let me start this tour, Buddy.

I thought you said you were sick, Mr. Disbig.

I was until I saw the doctor.

What did the doctor say was wrong with you?

Nothing is wrong with me. He said the creator of this book was to cheap to pay for color pages when he had the book published.

Well, he does have a family to support. Did you learn anything about the Doctor's House?

Yes I did, Buddy. The house was built in the 1870's at Main and Benton Streets in Santa Clara. It was rented to physicians and a dentist practiced in the back room. It was moved to the Museum in 1966. The medical instruments inside look really scary.

Good job, Mr. Disbig. Now let's go to the Portuguese Imperio House. I hear they have a beautiful altar on the first floor and the second floor has many historical exhibits.

Did you know the Compass Rose in front is made of granite? It was dedicated on Nov. 3, 2001 by the Portuguese Heritage Society of California. It's a replica of the 130-foot span in Lisbon, Portugal.

On June 7, 1997, Mr. Disbig, the Imperio was dedicated. It was during the first annual Portuguese festival. I advise everyone to stop in and learn the history. Let's cross the street and continue, Mr. Disbig.

Hey, Buddy. What are you doing?

I'm looking for Mr. Disbig, TedyCat.

I seen him walking over by the hotel.
He was looking a little pale.

Yeah. He mentioned something about
feeling faint. Is that Mr. Disbig?

I don't think so, Buddy. It looks
like a turkey.

Yeah. Right. Well, I'm going to continue
looking while I explain the Paulson
House. The house was built in the 1890's
and located at 343 Prevost St. in downtown
San Jose. I think I just saw Mr. Disbig.

That was a Turkey, Buddy. I'll explain the
Dashaway Stables if you want to go look
for Mr. Disbig, Buddy.

One more line, TedyCat. In 1986, the home
was moved to the History Park. The home
and family are still being researched as the
restoration process continues. Okay, TedyCat.

You want taxi service. You came to the right
place in 1888. Located at 130 S. Second Street
you could rent different types of vehicles to be
pulled by magnificent horses. One of the first
later on to provide reservation by phone service.
Come tour San Jose with excursions through the
beautiful valley. Rent a driver if needed.
Is that Mr. Disbig laying on the ground, Buddy?

I'm going to take a walk over and see
if that's him. It looks like it might be
a big hotdog they serve at O'Brien's
Candy store.

Hello, TedyCat. How are you?

I'm fine, Miss Nay Nay. Where's Buddy?

He's looking for Mr. Disbig. He sent me over to help you. Besides, I wanted to tour the Santa Anna School today.

Well, you are a school teacher for Kidstown School in our book, "The Adventures of Buddy the Clown and Mr. Disbig." But first, we need to walk along this path and visit the Greenwalt House.

That's right, and being a school teacher I know a little about the Greenwalt House. The house came to the History Park in 1991. It was built in 1877 in a Italianate farmhouse style, just North of Highway 85, and west of Almaden Expressway.

Very good, Miss NayNay. I guess I'll let you tell these fine visitors about the Santa Anna Schoolhouse while I go look for Buddy and Mr. Disbig.

Thank you, TedyCat. I'll see you in a little bit. Santa Anna School, it's beautiful. The wonderful teachings that went on in this 127 year old, one-room school after children walked for miles in the 1890's to get here had to be precious. Drinking water had to be brought in from neighbors with pails and the bathrooms, built from redwood, were then located in back of the school. Since there was a lack of schools at the time, more were built and San Jose had one of the first public schools.

Hola, Senorita NayNay. Good to see you. TedyCat sent me over to help you.

BigDaddy, good to see you again. You can help me tell the people about the Zanker House.

Si, Miss NayNay. It would be an honor. The house was built in the 1860's. William Zanker, from Germany, lived with his wife and 8 children in the home. In 1986, the house was moved to the History Park where it was restored. Out back is a 1906 redwood bathroom which was located on the original property at Zanker Road in Alviso.

Eight children. Wow. Now that's why we need schools. Thank you, BigDaddy.

You are very welcome, Senorita NayNay. And I must say, all of these homes are very special and I am proud to thank the people who have helped History Park maintain the preservation of this beautiful property.

I agree. This here is another of my favorite houses, BigDaddy. It is decorated inside with the 50's theme and furnished like my parents used to live. Michele Chiechi bought the home in 1913 and lived in it for 60 years. It was originally located at 820 Northrup Avenue when it was finally donated in 1973 to the Museum.

Hola, Senor Meegle, from the planet Mog. It is good to see you, amigo. What brings you to planet Earth?

Meegle visiting Pacific Ocean and all my fish friends tell Meegle, Buddy giving a tour of History Park and Meegle want to help.

Very good, amigo. Gracias. If you like, you can tell these wonderful folks the story of the Umbarger House.

Meegle like to tell story, thank you. In 1851 David Umbarger purchased 136.5 acres off Montery Road. He built this home in the 1870's. The land and home was left to his sister in 1891. The home arrived at the Museum in 1970.

Bravo, Senor Meegle. Would you like to tell another story?

Meegle would. Tell story Meegle know good. Meegle come from planet Mog...

No, Senor Meegle. Not your life story. The story of the Markham home.

Sorry, BigDaddy. Home Meegle think about. Poetry, children activities, library, readings, that's what the San Jose Center for Poetry and Literature use this home for among other delightful programs. Edwin Markham Land Association, in the 1920's, purchased the home. In 1987, it was moved to the History Park.

I think we should get off the trolley tracks before it comes, amigo.

Meegle, say hello to Rascoe. Rascoe good to see, Meegle like to know how are the many members of your family?

Meegle. My family is well. All twelve of them. Buddy sent me over to help you explain the Hill House.

Very good Hill House is. Explain, Rascoe, my friend, the legend of the Hill House.

Renowed photographer and artist, Andrew P. Hill, lived in this home at 1350 Sherman street in 1898. Some of his paintings are diplayed at the History Park. The Victorian Preservation Association sponsored the home and are currently restoring the structure. The home was moved to the History park in February 1997.

Tell a story Meegle want. Rascoe tell story good.

You can tell the next story, Meegle.

Meegle come from far far away...

No, Meegle. Perhaps later. Tell the story of the Post Office.

No mail Meegle get. Meegle like mail.

The Post Office story, Meegle.

Meegle love this story. Back in 1862, when stagecoaches traveled on the cattle trail between Santa Clara and San Francisco on Monterey road, this establishment served as both a bar and post office until 1882. It was the oldest working post office before it came to HSJ in 1972.

You know, they wanted young riders to ride horses from St. Louis to Sacramento to deliver the mail. Rabbits can run as fast as a horse at short distances.

Grapy. Good to see you. You're looking healthy.

I'm feeling healthy, Rascoe. Nothing like eating the proper foods to keep me trim and fit. Miss NayNay sent me over to help.

Great. I'll tell these wonderful folks about the Gordon House and you can tell them about Stevens Ranch Fruit Barn.

Okay. I love fruit. Wow. Did you see the size of that squirrel? I need to watch out for them. They eat all the good nuts that are healthy for me.

There's plenty of trees here at the History Park for everyone to enjoy. Did you know the author refers to this house as the Rotary Club home because the restoration was funded by the San Jose Rotary Club. They now use it as their headquarters?

No. I didn't. Wow. Look at that big squirrel.

The home was purchased by the Gordon family in 1887. Originally, the home sat at 5303 McKee Road. In 1986, the house was moved to the History Park.

Smell that fruit. Back in 1867, Orvis Stevens purchased the land where this fruit barn sat and by 1892, had grapes, pears, apples and peaches constituting one of the first orchards of Coyote Valley. He dried his fruit in this barn. The barn now houses displays of the past and the progress of Silicon Valley.
There's a squirrel on top of the barn, Rascoe.

We all need to eat. Let him be, Grapy.

Have you ever heard of a killer squirrel?

Hey, Slammer. What brings you to the History Park?

Buddy, sent me. I've come to save the day. I'm here to rescue those whom need to be rescued. I will fly high above and be on the lookout for those who need my help. I have come too...

Okay, okay. Just tell these fine folks about the Empire Firehouse.

I want to save someone.

You will. The Firehouse, Slammer.

In the 1800's Firehouse's were run by volunteers. After a city ordinance in 1854, professionals were required. In 1869, the Empire Firehouse was constructed due to an overwhelming demand of equipment storage space. The Empire Firehouse, located at 375 Second Street, housed the first fire engine of San Jose. A fire, in July of 1892, destroyed the building.

I liked that story. Good job. My turn now. The Electric Tower, as it was named, was the foresight of J.J. Owen. Not only did he want to light downtown San Jose, but he wanted to show others that San Jose was on the edge of modernization. The 237 foot, 24,000 candlepower tower, was ignited December 13, 1881, at the intersection of Santa Clara and Market Streets. A raging windstorm in February, 1915, brought the structure to its knees. This is a replica, standing 115 feet at the History Park.

Wow. I should've told that story. Oh well, too late. I still want to save something. Hey, Grapy. Look at that big squirrel.

Hi, Buddy. Did you find Mr. Disbig?

I was told he went in the hotel. I checked O'Brien's Candy store and the gift shop but could not find Mr. Disbig.

He's probably exploring the park. He'll be back. You want me to talk about the Bank of Italy?

Yeah. Go ahead, Slammer. Did you know the man sitting in the bank was the founder of the San Francisco Bank of Italy?

Amadeo Peter Giannini, in 1904, Buddy. In 1909, the first out of town branch opened. The bank was on the corner of Lightston and Santa Clara in downtown San Jose. Later on, he was to found the largest private bank, The Bank of America National Trust and Savings Association.

Quite a story, Slammer. Before I get to the Pacific Hotel, let's go inside to O'Brien's Candy Store where, in 1878, the first ice cream and soda's were served West of Detroit.

Yeah, I heard about that. In 1868, an Irish immigrant with $500.00 in his pocket, began selling baskets of candy outside the Pacific Hotel. His name was Maurice O'Brien and in 1874, moved to 30 S. First Street in downtown San Jose.

That's correct, Slammer. In 1880, the original Pacific Hotel was at 74-80 South Market Street. This hotel had reading rooms, billiard halls, bath and bar. And I'm sure this is really what the visitors want to hear. $1.00 to $1.50, room and board.

Hey, Mr. Disbig. Where have you been?

I wasn't feeling so well. I went to the Pacific Hotel.

I didn't see you there. Slammer and I just had an
ice cream at O'Brien's Candy Store.

I was up in the conference room sleeping.

Well, you want to talk about the print shop?

No. No. No more talk about black and white. I think
I'll cross the street to the Ng Shing Gung Temple
and take in all its beauty and magnificent exhibits.

Okay, Mr. Disbig. I'll meet you there after I
talk about the print shop. This structure was
built in 1884. Originally located at North San
Pedro and St. John Streets in downtown San
Jose, the false front of this building was
characteristic of old buildings in San Jose.
In 1972, the building was moved to HSJ.

That was quick, Buddy. I guess I'll talk about
"Ng Shing Gung," when translated means;
"Temple of Five Gods." The original building
was demolished in 1949, but the altar, the five
divinities; God of Wealth, Goddess of Mercy,
Queen of Heaven, the Canton City God and
God of War and Justice were preserved. They
are part of the beautiful exhibits preserved by
The Chinese Historical and Cultural Project.

Come on, Mr. Disbig. Let's get you some gas and then go shoe a horse.

I really don't feel like shoeing a horse. What ever that means, Buddy

That's okay, Mr. Disbig. I'll explain the story of this Associated Gas Station which sat on the corner of Julian and Market Streets in downtown San Jose in 1927. Owned by different private parties throughout the years, it was finally scheduled to be torn down. With the help of volunteers, the building was saved, and in 1978, moved to the History Park.

What kind of ice cream did you have, Buddy?

Strawberry.

I like Rainbow Sherbet.

Do you want an ice cream, Mr. Disbig?

Yeah.

Let me tell the story of the Blacksmith and then we'll get a ice cream before we ride the trolley.

The trolley. Forget the ice cream, Buddy. I want to ride the trolley. Can I ride the trolley? Can I? Can I?

Sure, Mr. Disbig. Give me a moment. The Blacksmith shop was used to repair wagons, shoe horses, make tools and other instruments from iron and steel forged over hot coals. Sometimes they have exhibitions in this shed during festivals at the History Park.

Can I ride the trolley now?

Yes.

Oh, goody.

Hello, Miss NayNay and TedyCat. I guess everyone wants to ride the trolley. Let me tell these wonderful folks about the history of the Trolley Barn and trolley number 143, also known as the Birney.

Hurry up, Buddy. I want to ride the trolley.

Mr. Disbig, let Buddy tell the story.

You be nice to Mr. Disbig, TedyCat. He just wants to ride the trolley. It's okay, Mr. Disbig.

Thank you, Miss NayNay. I'll buy you an ice cream.

Okay, everyone. Anyway. This Trolley Barn was built in 1984. It was built in the tradition of California Barns from the early 1900's. Inside are projects which have been restored with the help of volunteers and the California Trolley and Railroad Corporation (www.ctrc.org). Two of the trolley cars are used here at the park. They plan, hopefully, to extend the trolley tracks to link Kelley Park. This trolley car, #143, ran in Fresno. The St. Louis Car Co. built this in 1922 and was designed to have a single operator. The name Birney, came from the designer, Mr. Charles Birney.

Can we ride now? I want to get on before Mr. Disbig.

One more page, TedyCat. Do I get a soda with my ice cream, Mr. Disbig?

De Luz   Pasetta   Doctor's Office   Portuguese Imperio

Paulson   Dashaway Stables   Greenwalt   Santa Anna School

Zanker   Chiechi   Umbarger   Markham

Andrew P. Hill   Post Office   Gordon   Fruit Barn

Firehouse   Electric Light Tower   Bank of Italy   Pacific Hotel

Ng Shing Gung Temple   Print Shop   Gas Station   Blacksmith

Trolley Barn   Visit www.historysanjose.org   Birney #143

34

Hey, Grapy. Leave those squirrels alone.

Thanks, Slammer. Hello, everyone. I'm sure you remember all my friends from today. If you would like to see more of them visit your bookstore and ask for ISBN number 1-4010-9050-8 or just ask for "The Adventures of Buddy the clown and Mr. Disbig." You can also visit www.prtproductions.com and save time and money.

Enough about us. We like to think of the History Park as one of the most informative, beautiful, peaceful and serene parks we have had the pleasure to visit. Voted family favorite in 2005 by Bay Area Parent. The History Park provides an ambience of joy and relaxation along with many special events provided to the public.

Here you are openly greeted to a family atmosphere of fun while you learn about days that were before many of us were born. Not only does the History Park offer times from the past, it allows new ones for the future with you in mind.

The pleasure you receive from the staff and from very well-trained and energetic volunteers is overwhelming. Their goal is to please the public and they show that desire by helping everyone to understand these buildings history. If not for these great people along with you, parks like these may not flourish. We invite all of you to come visit the park everyday when the park is open. Either come by yourself or with your family. Visit the events the park has to offer or book your own family event.

We have given you brief descriptions of the buildings at the park to find out more come visit HSJ in person or at www.historysanjose.org. Thank you for your time. Now it's time to introduce another of our favorite parks at Kelly Park; the Japanese Friendship Gardens.

Can we ride the trolley now, Buddy?

I still want my ice cream, Mr. Disbig.

Japanese Friendship Gardens at Kelly Park

Six and a half acres of Kelley Park was dedicated as a home for the Japanese Friendship Gardens in 1960. Okayama's world famous Korakuen Garden was used as the design to create the warm atmosphere while placing bridges, rocks, trees and flowers to establish a serene setting. Visitors marvel at the spectacular and breath taking appearance of the park which came together from visitor's like you and other contributions from numerous organizations.

On the 8th anniversary of the Sister City affiliation, in 1965, the Japanese Friendship Garden was dedicated. Keeping with the dream, which started in 1957, when President Eisenhower wished to establish a relationship between other countries and the United States.

The Pacific Neighbors, an organization formed to sponsor as a link between the two-cities, made the original proposed concept to create the Japanese Friendship Gardens.

Inside the park you will see beautiful attractions stemming from a waterfall to trees, bridges, lanterns, a Pagoda, Teahouse, Turtle Island and plenty of Koi fish. Read everything you find because inside this beautiful park, everything not only has a story, but a special meaning as well. Come visit the park and enjoy the traquil leisure the park offers. For more information go to www.ci.san-jose.ca.us/cae/parks

A Haiku poem

I've changed my dwelling
To bathe in Summer coolness
So tranquil, so calm.
—— Paul Iwashita

Happy Hollow Park and Zoo at Kelley Park

In 1961, Happy Hollow opened the doors to become one of San Jose's favorite children's parks and zoo. Surrounded by the community and nestled under beautiful shade trees, this family park offers the public an incredible journey from fabulous picnic areas to marionette puppet shows and maybe the most popular of amusement rides, Danny the Dragon Train. Built by the Arrow Development Co. in 1960 and credited with rides such as Dumbo in Disneyland, this machine shop started with a group of World War II veterans.

Rare and endangered species survive at this accredited institution along with a petting zoo which offers a variety of goats, a Dwarf Zebu, Llamas and other fun creatures for the children to interact with while learning the history behind these very special animals.

Happy Hollow's 12.5 acre park offers a variety of activities stemming from birthday parties to educational programs including summer camp for children. This moderatly priced park and zoo has playgrounds for the entire family to enjoy and offers many special events like Earth Day Celebration and Annual Food Drive.

We are proud to have given you information concerning these favorite family gathering places here at Kelley Park and invite you to come visit these fine facilities which will be able to provide more information of the guidelines set forth to enjoy all the ammenities they have to offer. Not only does Kelley Park have three tremendous establishments inside the park, additionally it offers the Leininger Center, which can provide you with information on reserving other attractive San Jose Regional Parks. Now let's visit two other fantastic museums and then some of those other family parks. Please, get out of the water, Meegle.

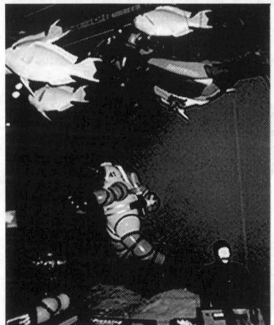

The Tech Museum of Innovation is located at 201 South Market Street in San Jose. The three-level facility houses' 132,000-square feet of fun and technology for the entire family, young and old alike, to not only play with some of the most remarkable gadgets but to learn from them as well.

The Tech Museum of Innovation started in 1978, as an inspiration to bring science and technology together for human awareness. Junior League of Palo Alto had a vision to create such a project and later, teamed with the San Jose League to initiate its goals. In 1990, a 20,000- square foot test center opened at the old Convention Center and proven successful has been given a warm reception by visitors alike and a standing ovation from the citizens of Silicon Valley.

Over 2,800,000 visitors have come to see the phenomenal building home to unprecedented exhibits. Workshops and labs allow the visitor to explore leisurely during their adventure while others get involved with the learning potential. "The mind is a limitless void, capable of drawing in and out."

A projected 650,000 each year are expected to visit the creative and gallant structure with a Domed Imax® Theater, a cafe, bookstore, gift shop, educational center and one-of-a-kind exhibits. This infrastructure fills the hearts with progress and capabilities set forth by human nature and the desire to not only learn but to continue to learn and invent for not only today or tomorrow, but for the next generations to come.

Exciting opportunities happen at the Tech Museum of Innovation including awards that were inspired by individuals who developed particular goals. In 2001, the awards were brought forth to accompany the achievement of not only individuals, but also new an old companies wanting to better the world. Awards for environment. Awards for education. Awards for economics, health, communication, agriculture, medicine, jobs, poverty, equality. These are only a small percentage given out each year; more awards can be documented for individual commitments.

The Tech Museum of Innovation has opened a door to progress and with the help of individuals like you can continue its dreams of becoming a learning institution for everyone. Become a member and dwell in the satisfaction that with every little contribution, the world is becoming a better place to live.

BUDDY

*Pictures from Hubble - Credit: Nasa

The Tech Museum of Innovation

New-TechTag pilot program personalizes your visit. View your adventure online.

Most of us believe learning should be fun, others think if it's that easy, it's not right. The Tech Museum of Innovation grants you the ability to have fun while you learn. Everything from robotics to exploration of sciences is offered to enhance self-knowledge and awareness.

Visit the Earthquake Platform Shake and shimmy to an 8.4

One of the best ways to learn is to interact; the Tech Museum of Innovation does just that, not only for adults but also for children. One of the most precious sounds you could hear is the laughter of children. Now you can listen to the children laugh as they make their way through the Play Path, an exhibition of discovery and enrichment for the young.

Create your own reality world.

Imagination playground invites the children to learn while they have fun with Glow Stones, a new version of wood blocks responding to signals from other stones. Toy Boxes; learn technology from within the box. Sneak and Spies, clubhouses, one high one low, watch the kids as they listen and spy around the exhibits. Bug Puppets, Shadow Garden and Maraca Motion, these fun adventurous interactives allow first hand knowledge of creativity.

Imagination Playground

The future is bright for all of us and with learning centers like this one. It is a future of excitement for every city, for every person, for the endowment of life that can be carried out to inspire, aspire and create a separate vision for each and everyone of us.
For information call: 408-294-Tech or visit www.thetech.org.

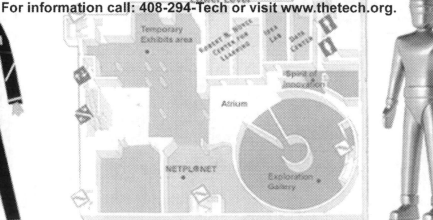

*Map provided at The Tech Museum of Innovation

Children's Discovery Museum

Hello, my name's Jack. My brother Buddy wanted me to introduce a very important Museum to everyone. A museum I recently visited called The Children's Discovery Museum. The museum is fantastic.

I was surprised and inspired on how well the museum was set up for the children. And, I saw how every child there was having a delightful good time. They were laughing, playing, jumping and participating in all the activities the museum had to offer.

On the first floor they have WaterWays, these magnificent water games let the children experiment with colorful plastic balls as they invade the water sources and perform to the different actions from the water. They do supply splash gear for the children.

They also have, Bubbalogna, which allows children and adults to experiment with bubbles. They have Current Connections, Kids Garden, Post Office, Rhythm Huts, Step into the Past, Streets, Take Another Look, The Lee and Diane Bradenburg Theater and Zoomzone™ and this is all on the first floor.

On the second floor they have Pizza Please, CdMedia.studio and a wonderful exhibit named, The Wonder Cabinet, a perfect learning center with a responsible staff that allows infants and preschoolers to learn hands on exploring of basic fundamentals. Overall, I can understand why Children's Discovery Museum has won many awards.

I was able to take some pictures of my tour and I would like to share them with you along with a little history that I believe is important, so turn the page and enjoy what I enjoyed. By the way, The Children's Discovery Museum has a large facility which can be used to accommodate almost any party. To find out more call (408) 298-5437 or visit their website at www.cdm.org. Better yet, take a little drive with the family to 180 Woz Way in San Jose, Ca. 95110

A place where the child must feel that the whole plant is for him, that the best is offered to him because of faith in his power to use it, that he has access to all departments, and that he is always a welcome visitor, never an intruder.
Anna Billings Gallup

* Establishment of board of Directors, September, 1982.
* Establishment of a permanent site with approval (December 1984) by the San Jose Redevelopment Agency of funding allocation to aquire property for the Museum within the Guadalupe River Park.

* Implementation of a comprehensive "Museum on the Road" program, encompassing "Stage Door Stories" (1984) and a traveling exhibit on disabilities, "One Way or Another" (1985) serving more than 40,000 children to date.

* Commencement of exhibit fabrication by Museum staff January, 1988.
* Completion of Capital Campaign, July, 1989 with more than $9.75 million raised.

* Occupancy of the 42,000 square foot facility, January, 1990, designed by internationally renowned architect Ricardo Legorreta of Legorreta Arquitectos, who was also commissioned to design the Quadalupe River Park.

* Celebration of Children's Discovery Museum's public opening, June 2 and 3, 1990.

National Awards:
* Most Promissing Pratices Award 2000- Awarded by Met Life Foundation and the Association of Children's Museums recognizing our Summer of Service program.

* National Award for Museum and Library Service- Awarded by the Institute for Museum and Library Services, the highest honor a museum or library can receive for service to its community.

Recognition:
* Child Magazine (2002), "Top Ten Children's Museums"

CHILDREN'S DISCOVERY MUSEUM

Alum Rock Park

Located off Alum Rock Ave. in San Jose, this diverse park offers a family friendly atmosphere with plenty of childrens activities including a museum identifying certain wildlife, plants and floral. Comprised of 700-acres, which include biking trails, walking trails and picnic areas, slides and swings meet the need for children with a nice area for hikers, roller blades and bicyclists. There is a fee attached for cars but you can walk in or bike in free of charge. For more information call: 408-277-5561

Anderson Lake

Located at 19245 Malaquerra Ave. in Morgan Hill, sits 3,109 acres, Santa Clara's largest reservoir, with multiple trails. Power and non-power boats are welcome on the seven-mile long lake and even jet-skis skim by on the placid waters. This beautiful scenic park offers, fishing, picnic areas and barbecue facilities for the entire family to enjoy right on the shoreline. Equestrians use the park along with bicyclists and everyone can enjoy a nice swim on a hot day. For information call: 408-779-3634

Almaden Quicksilver Mines

A landmark of California history, the 4,147 acres offers beautiful wildflowers and 34.2 miles of hiking trails and also a history of over 135 years of mining. Located in the town of New Almaden in South San Jose, the quicksilver (mercury) mines had made fish in the area unsafe to eat. Mining structures throughout the park have been sealed and gates locked. However, comprised of equestrian trails, walking trails, bike trails, a museum and picnic tables, you are still invited to walk your dog. For more information call: 408-268-3883

Calero County Park

Located at 23201 McKean Road in San Jose, the 3,476 acre park offers a breath-taking look at the California Oak woodland. Immersed with beautiful plants and natural wildlife, the recreational activities include sailing, fishing, boating, water and jet-skiing. 18.6 miles are available to hike. Picnic and barbecues span the water's edge. Horse rentals are available at the Calero Ranch Stables. For more information call: 408-268-3883

Chesbro Reservoir County Park

Located at 17655 Oak Glen Road near Morgan Hill, the 216 acre park and man-made reservoir is a haven for fisherman. Black Bass, Catfish, Crappie, Trout and Large Mouth Bass swim in the cool waters where only non-powered boats are allowed. Beautiful calm waters set the theme for sailboats and kayaking. The park has established no designated trails. For more information call: 408-779-9232

Ed R. Levin County Park

Situated at 3100 Calaveras Rd. in Milpitas, golfing, picnicking and fishing are recreational events at this 1,539 acre park. Gorgeous lawn areas stretch through the park making it family friendly while nature-lovers hike and bike through beautiful Oak woodlands. Watch the hang-gliders and paragliders while you fish or sail one of your model sailboats from an inflatable raft. Relaxation is what the park offers with its 19 miles of trails.
For information call: 408-262-6980

Hellyer County Park

Located at 985 Hellyer Ave. in San Jose, this beautiful 205 acre park offers an Olympic-size bicycle racetrack Coyote Creek runs through the park that allows the visitor to explore a scenic route along paved trails. Fishing, hiking and play areas are just a few of the amenities along with grasslands to throw a frisbee or have a barbecue.
For information call: 408-225-0225

Joseph D. Grant

Situated at 18405 Mt. Hamilton Rd. in San Jose sits the largest regional park in Santa Clara County. Beautiful oak trees abound surrounding some of the finest landscaped recreational areas on this 9,553 acre park. Watch the cattle craze, ride a horse, have a picnic or take in a leisurely hike choosing from 52 trails. Several small ponds and a large lake are what the fisherman dream. Reserve one of forty family campsites.
For information call: 408-274-6121

Lake Cunningham Regional Park

Two entrances open into this park, one on White Rd. and the other off Tully Rd. in San Jose. This beautiful 202 acre scenic park was opened in 1982 for family fun and leisure. Rent a paddle boat, a canoe or even a sailboat and explore the 50 acre fresh water lake. Harboring a fitness course, bike trail and walking trail along with picnic areas, this park entertains everyone from young to old. Throw a line in and see if there's bluegill, bass or catfish on the other end. Visit Raging Waters next door where waterslides are the attraction. For information call: 408-277-5351

Lexington Reservoir County Park

Located at 17770 Alma Bridge Rd. in Los Gatos just off Hwy. 17, a 475 acre man-made lake sits awaiting the next fisherman. Available to non-gas powerboats only, you can still launch a rowboat, sailboards or electric powered boats. The 941 acre park provides walking trails that may ultimatly connect to several other parks.
For more information call: 408-356-2729

*Map provided at www.parkhere.org

Mt. Madonna County Park

Located at 7850 Pole Line Rd. in Watsonville and surrounded by a beautiful majestic redwood forest, this 3,688 acre park overlooks Monterey Bay. Nestled with grassy meadows and scenic trails, descendants of the White fallow deer, which were donated in 1932 by William Randolph Hearst, wander in an enclosed area for the public to view. Reserve a campsite and have a family barbecue or visit the archery range. Listen to live music at the amphitheater or learn about Indians, nature and cultural history at the visitor's center. Drive in with your RV and relax the nights away.
For more information call: 408-842-2341

Santa Teresa County Park

Nestled above Santa Teresa Golf Course in San Jose, this 1,627 acre park hosts a beautiful spectrum for ecology lovers. Picnic tables and barbecue areas provide relaxation for your group while others may want to ride a horse. Visit the archery range or climb on board a golf cart while visiting the 18- hole course. For more information call: 408-225-2650

Uvas Canyon County Park

Situated at 8515 Croy Rd. in Morgan Hill and housing, twenty-five campsites, the 1,133 acres offers miles of hiking trails while some visit natures waterfalls. Smell the aroma of the spectacular flora while enjoying a nice family picnic. Visit Uvas or Chesbro reservoirs during your stay and explore on a non-powered boat. For information call: 408-779-9232

Vasona Lake County Park and
the Los Gatos Creek Parkway

Located at 333 Blossom Hill Rd. in San Jose, a wonderful very family-oriented, 150 acre park looms, inviting visitors to explore all its highlights and beauty. Come paddle a boat, row one, fish, hike, jog or ride a bike along the trails with your dog. This fantastic park has a lot for everyone. Take the children to the playgrounds and ride a carousel, a merry-go-round or ride the Billy Jones Wildcat Railroad. Come have a picnic and throw a ball, kick a ball or settle down and relax with a fishing pole while you observe the parks waterfowl. For more information call: 408-356-2729

*Map provided at www.parkhere.org

"Red Rose" By Paul Trainer 12/21/98 (HillTop Records)
She is standing there with a ribbon in her hair and
in her right hand a red rose.
She looks to see what it all means as she looks at the ground below.
Her dreams were filled with loving him knowing they would never end.
You can see a tear fall from her eye as the memories dance, through her mind.
To touch your hand.
To hold you tight.
To kiss your soft lips once again.
My memories of loving you keep dancing through my mind.
I wonder why they took you away
Just to bring you back this way
The world is good I know in my heart but why did loving have to start
I hear your voice in the middle of the night and hope to wake by your side
To touch your hand.
To hold you tight.
To kiss your soft lips once again.
She is standing there with a ribbon in her hair and in her right hand a red rose.
She looks to see what it all means as she leans over the gray stone
Her dreams were filled with loving him knowing they would never end.
Her hearts at ease and her minds at peace as she drops, her red rose
To touch your hand.
To hold you tight.
To kiss your soft lips once again.
My memories of loving you keep dancing through my mind.

"Fish in the Ocean" Paul Trainer 1983
Golden yellow glitter in the trees, a tall thin man standing by the sea
watching for the sunrise alone in the dark with not much time
Holding everything that is true he dreamed of living with someone like you
but he found out late, now has his doubts, for where he goes no one will know
Fish in the ocean, the moon in the sky, watching for the sunrise
The deep blue ocean is his escape and as the tides roll in they break against the rocks
Time has passed it goes so fast and the seagulls fly so free
Fish in the ocean, the moon in the sky
watching for the sunrise

"Little child on the front line" Paul Trainer 1983
Oh little child on the front line
get off the beach while you still can
the sounds of gunfire coming from all sides
stop the war there's no more reason to die
Oh little child on the front line
the beach is glowing in the moonlight
the sands are covered with bloodshed
get out of site before you are dead
Oh little child on the front line
your mama's crying for you to be found
There's bodies laying to the left and the right
let us hope you escape this night
Oh little child on the front line
with the bombs bursting in the night sky
the sound of shells exploding on the ground
it's great to know America is still around
Oh little child on the front line
you were found still alive
your mama's waiting for you to come home
Oh little child your no longer alone

"Don't give up" by Paul Trainer 1981
When your feeling
your about to give up
when your road is getting
to rough
don't lose your hold on life
because you can take it on in
strides
When your woman she leaves
when you lose her love
and you can't get it back
you got to stay on the right track
Don't give up
No, don't give up
Don't lose, your hold on life
You can live a life of your own
but you must take control
you got to move with the flow
and you can't let go
When you feel your body tremble
in the middle of the night
and you dream of life and
how you held her tight
Don't give up
No, don't give up
Don't lose, your hold on life.

"Moondog over Miami" Paul Trainer 1984
She came out of the fog diffferent from mankind
it was worse then someone could describe
She had four claws walked on two
a sight that would boggle the mind
Moondog, Moondog, Moondog
Moondog over Miami
Heard of her existence from rumors in the night
said she came in and devoured at sight
Moondog, Moondog
Her skin was red she looked like the dead
eyes of doom when she looked at you
Moondog, Moondog, Moondog
Moondog over Miami
She had control of any man she held
stole his soul and crushed his bones
Showed no feelings had no heart
grown men would scream running through the park
Moondog, Moondog, Moondog
Moondog over Miami
She would fight lions and tame the bears
eyes of doom when she looked at you
Moondog
Moondog over Miami

Qty	Description	Price	*S/H	**Ins.	Total
	Buddy the Clown book Signed	$27.00	$3.00		
	Buddy Poster	$20.00	$3.00		
	Buddy Poster Signed	$30.00	$3.00		
	Buddy Fan Club Signed	$5.00	$2.00		
	Buddy Friends Faces Poster	$20.00	$3.00		
	Buddy Friends Faces Poster Signed	$30.00	$3.00		
	Clown Novel Signed	$25.00	$3.00		
*Sold in Bulk	*Learning the History of Kelley Park in San Jose	Inquire at prtproductions @hotmail.com	$.00		
	Learning the History of Kelley Park in San Jose Signed by Author	$20.00	$3.00		
	Screenplays	$500,000.	Free		
	1 Song -8x10- sheet Song Lyrics -Signed	$5.00 Each	$3.00		

Message: | Write song or songs in message | Total

Send Check or Money order to:

PRT Productions

3697 Norwood Ave.

San Jose, Ca. 95148

Ship to:

Name:

Street Address:

City:

State:

*S/H- $3.00 per item   **Insurance (optional) $1.50 per item

Money order ship next day Checks wait to clear

Free S/H for Orders over $60.00

Order inquiry prtproductions@hotmail.com

Prices subject to change. CA. TAX Rate.

Copy and print shipping form for order.
Send with check or money order
Order online at www.prtproductions.com

Printed in the United States
By Bookmasters